SO-FAH-901

The Perfect Gift – DIY Mason Jar Gift Recipes

25 Mason Jar Recipes to Make the Perfect Gift

BY

MOLLY MILLS

Copyright © 2019 by Molly Mills

License Notes

No part of this book may be copied, replicated, distributed, sold or shared without the express and written consent of the Author.

The ideas expressed in the book are for entertainment purposes. The Reader assumes all risk when following any guidelines and the Author accepts no responsibility if damages occur due to actions taken by the Reader.

An Amazing Offer for Buying My Book!

Thank you very much for purchasing my books! As a token of my appreciation, I would like to extend an amazing offer to you! When you have subscribed with your e-mail address, you will have the opportunity to get free and discounted e-books that will show up in your inbox daily. You will also receive reminders before an offer expires so you never miss out. With just little effort on your part, you will have access to the newest and most informative books at your fingertips. This is all part of the VIP treatment when you subscribe below.

SIGN ME UP: *https://molly.gr8.com*

Table of Contents

Chapter I: Dessert Mason Jar Gift Recipes

AAAAAAAAAAAAAAAAAAAAAAAAAAAAAAAAAAAAAAAAAAAAAAAA

Recipe 1: Cinnamon and Spice Muffin Mix Mason Jar Gift

These cinnamon spice muffins are delicious no matter what the time of year, but are especially welcomed when the weather turns cold and the snow starts to fall.

Yield: 1 Gift Jar

Cooking Time: 20 minutes

List of Ingredients:

- ¾ cup granulated sugar
- 2 ½ cups flour, all-purpose
- 2 tsp. baking powder
- ½ tsp. baking soda
- ½ tsp. table salt
- ½ cup packed brown sugar
- ¼ tsp. ginger, ground
- 1 ½ tsp. cinnamon, ground
- ¼ tsp. cloves, ground
- ¼ tsp. nutmeg, ground
- Twine

- Cupcake liners
- Baggie
- Quart-sized Mason jar

AAAAAAAAAAAAAAAAAAAAAAAAAAAAAAAAAAAAAAAAAAAAAAAAAA

Instructions:

1: Mix 1 cup of the flour with the baking powder, baking soda, cinnamon, sugar, nutmeg, cloves and ginger together. Pour this mixture into the jar.

2: Mix the brown sugar with the remaining flour and pour into a baggie. Secure the baggie close and place directly on top of the mixture inside the Mason jar.

3: Attach the lid and ring on the Mason jar. Secure the cupcake liners with twin to the jar. Place the following instructions on the jar:

1. Turn the oven on to 400 degrees.
2. Open the baggie and pour into a bowl. Mix in ¼ cup butter. This is the muffin's crumb topping. Place the bowl to the side.
3. Mix in 1 cup milk, 1 tsp. vanilla extract, ¼ cup vegetable oil and 1 large egg.
4. Place the cupcake liners into the muffin tin. Spoon the mixture into the lined muffin tin.
5. Evenly sprinkle the crumb topping from 2 on the top of the batter.
6. Bake for 15 minutes or until a toothpick inserted in the middle comes out clean.

Recipe 2: Chex Mix Gift Jar

This no-bake gift jar mix is simple and quick to throw together, and can be customized to fit the holiday or occasion. For example, you can make the mix have a Christmassy vibe by using a bag of holiday M&Ms (red and green) instead of the traditional bag.

Yield: 1 Gift Jar

Cooking Time: 15 minutes

List of Ingredients:

- Decorative fabric
- Twine or ribbon
- 1 box chocolate Chex Mix cereal
- 1 bag plain M&Ms
- 1 bag Chex Mix Muddy Buddies
- 1 bag mini pretzel twists
- Mason jar

AAAAAAAAAAAAAAAAAAAAAAAAAAAAAAAAAAAAAAAAAAAAAAAA

Instructions:

1: Open the bag of Chex Mix Muddy Buddies and pour it into a large bowl. Do the same with the bag of M&Ms, Chex Mix cereal and pretzel twists. Stir the mixture together until everything is blended well.

2: Carefully pour the Chex Mix mixture into the clean Mason jar. Place the lid on top of the jar.

3: Cut out a 5 to 6-inch diameter circle from the decorative fabric. Place the circle directly on top of the lid and secure the ring over the fabric and down onto the jar.

4: Tie a pretty bow around the jar using the twin or decorative ribbon. If you're giving the mix-filled jar as a Holiday gift, attach a candy cane to the jar with the twin or ribbon.

Recipe 3: Banana Bread with Chocolate Chip Mix Mason Gift Jar

There is little that can make banana bread better, except for chocolate! The combination of chocolate chips and bananas creates a delicious bread that will please everyone in your family.

Yield: 1 Gift Jar

Cooking Time: 12 minutes

List of Ingredients:

- 2 ½ cups Bisquick
- 1 tsp. baking powder
- ¼ tsp. table salt
- ½ cups dried bananas, chopped finely
- ½ cup granulated sugar
- ½ cup mini or regular-sized chocolate chips

AAAAAAAAAAAAAAAAAAAAAAAAAAAAAAAAAAAAAAAAAAAAAAAAAA

Instructions:

1: Mix the baking powder, salt and Bisquick together. Pour it into the jar.

2: Add the granulated sugar on top of the mixture from 1, followed by the chocolate chips and the dried bananas.

3: Secure the Mason jar close and attach the following Instructions:

1. Lightly grease a loaf pan. Lay a piece of wax paper along the bottom of the pan. Set the pan to the side.
2. Turn the oven on and preheat to 350 degrees.
3. Dump the contents of the Mason jar into a mixing bowl. Add 2 slightly beaten large eggs, 1 ¼ cup milk. 1 tsp. vanilla extract and ½ cup of butter softened at room temperature. Mix all the ingredients together.
4. Spread the batter evenly into the loaf pan. Place in the oven and bake for about 1 hour. When a toothpick that is inserted in the middle comes out clean, the bread is done.

Recipe 4: Blondie Toffee Bars Mason Jar Gift Mix

While similar but completely different from brownies, blondies are a dessert set

Yield: 1 Gift Jar

Cooking Time: 15 minutes

List of Ingredients:

- 1 cup flour, all-purpose
- 1 tsp. baking powder
- ¼ tsp. table salt
- 1 cup packed brown sugar
- ½ cup chocolate chips, mini
- ¾ cup Rice Krispie cereal
- ½ cup toffee chips
- Quart-sized Mason jar

AAAAAAAAAAAAAAAAAAAAAAAAAAAAAAAAAAAAAAAAAAAAAAAAAA

Instructions:

1: Mix the all-purpose flour, baking powder and table salt together. Pour this mixture into the jar.

2: Add the brown sugar on top of the flour mixture. Place the mini chocolate chips on top of the brown sugar, followed by the Rice Krispie cereal and finally the toffee chips.

3: Secure the lid and ring onto the jar and attach the following Instructions:

1. Grease lightly an 8x8-inch pan. Turn on the oven and preheat at 350 degrees.
2. Beat 2 large eggs lightly in a mixing bowl. Add 1 tsp. of vanilla extract and ¼ cup of butter softened at room temperatures. Lightly beat the mixture until it becomes smooth and fluffy.
3. Dump the contents of the jar into the mixture. Stir together until well combined.
4. Evenly spread the mixture into the greased 8x8-inch pan. Place in the oven and back for about 30 minutes.

Chapter II: Chocolate Mason Jar Gift Recipes

AAAAAAAAAAAAAAAAAAAAAAAAAAAAAAAAAAAAAAAAAAAAAAAA

Recipe 5: Adult Hot Cocoa Mason Jar Gift Recipe

This isn't your children's hot cocoa. In fact, this hot cocoa recipe contains alcohol so don't give this gift jar to anyone under the age of 21.

Yield: 1 Gift Jar

Cooking Time: 10 minutes

List of Ingredients:

- Hot chocolate mix packets
- Bailey's, individual alcohol bottle
- Mini marshmallows
- Mason jar
- Ribbon

AAAAAAAAAAAAAAAAAAAAAAAAAAAAAAAAAAAAAAAAAAAAAAAAAA

Instructions:

1: Open the hot chocolate mix packets and dump into the Mason jar. You want the jar to be about half full of the hot cocoa.

2: Pour the mini marshmallows on top of the hot cocoa until there is no more room in the Mason jar.

3: Place the lid and ring on the jar. Attach the bottle of Bailey's alcohol with the ribbon.

Recipe 6: M&M Delight Cookie Mix

Who doesn't love M&Ms? This delicious cookie mix will create a yummy M&M cookie that will please anyone.

Yield: 1 Gift Jar

Cooking Time: 15 minutes

List of Ingredients:

- 1 ¼ cup plain M&Ms
- 1 ¼ cup sugar, granulated
- 2 cups all-purpose flour
- ½ tsp. baking soda
- ½ tsp. baking powder
- Quart-sized Mason jar, wide-mouth

AAAAAAAAAAAAAAAAAAAAAAAAAAAAAAAAAAAAAAAAAAAAAAAAAAA

Instructions:

1: Combine the flour, baking soda and baking powder together. Set to the side.

2: Carefully pour the sugar into the Mason jar. Add the plain M&Ms into the jar and onto the sugar.

3: Pour the mixture from 1 into the jar. You should now have a jar with the sugar, M&Ms and flour mixture layered.

4: Attach the Mason jar lid and ring and secure closed.

5: Place a piece of decorative fabric over the top of the jar's lid and tie with a cute ribbon.

6: Attach the following recipe to the jar: Combine 1 large egg, ½ tsp. vanilla and ½ cup of butter. Add the ingredients in the jar and mix until well-combined. Scoop the dough onto a cookie sheet and bake at 350-degrees for 11 minutes.

Recipe 7: S'Mores Mason Gift Jar

S'Mores are a campfire favorite that doesn't require the hassle of camping in order to enjoy their deliciousness.

Yield: 1 Gift Jar

Cooking Time: 10 minutes

List of Ingredients:

- 1 package mini marshmallows
- 1 ½ cups graham crackers, crushed
- 1 ¼ cup plain M&Ms or chocolate chips
- 1/3 cup packed brown sugar
- Quart-sized Mason jar

AAAAAAAAAAAAAAAAAAAAAAAAAAAAAAAAAAAAAAAAAAAAAAAAAAA

Instructions:

1: Pour the crushed graham crackers directly into the jar. Pack the graham crackers tightly into the bottom of the jar. A meat tenderizer works well for this job.

2: Add about 2/3 of the marshmallows on top of the crushed crackers. Press the marshmallows up against the sides of the jar so that there is a well or hole in the middle of the marshmallow layer.

3: Pour the brown sugar into the hole or well you created in the middle of the marshmallow layer. Press the brown sugar gently down a bit using your fingers.

4: Add the M&Ms or chocolate chips into the jar. Place the lid and ring on the jar to secure it closed.

5: Add some decorations, such as ribbon and fabric, to the jar and attach a tag with the following bakinInstructions:

1. Preheat the oven to 350 degrees and lightly grease a pan measuring 9x9. Set the pan to the side for the moment.
2. Pour the contents of the jar into a bowl and mix thoroughly until all ingredients are well blended.
3. In a separate bowl, combine 1/3 cup milk, ½ cup melted butter and 1 tsp. vanilla extract.
4. Stir the milk and butter mixture into the dry ingredient mixture until all ingredients are well combined.
5. Press the batter into the lightly greased pan from 1. Place the pan in the oven and bake until done, which is about 15 minutes.

Recipe 8: Brownie Cake Mason Jar Gift Recipe

This gift jar recipe combines brownie and cake to create a gift jar that any chocolate-lover will want.

Yield: 2 Gift Jars

Cooking Time: 60 minutes

List of Ingredients:

- 1 cup white sugar
- 1 cup all-purpose flour
- ¼ tsp. cinnamon
- ½ tsp. baking soda
- 3 Tbsp. cocoa powder, unsweetened
- 1/3 cup butter
- ¼ cup buttermilk
- ¼ cup lukewarm water
- ½ tsp. real or imitation vanilla extract
- 1 large egg, beaten
- ¼ cups walnuts, finely chopped
- 2 Mason jars, pint-sized & wide-mouth

AA

Instructions:

1: Preheat the oven to 325-degrees.

2: Whisk the baking soda, cinnamon, sugar and flour together. Set to the side.

3: Cream the butter, water and unsweetened cocoa powder together in a saucepan. Place on the stove and heat over low until the butter is completely melted. Make sure to stir the entire time to prevent the ingredients from burning. Once everything is well blended, remove the saucepan from heat.

4: Carefully stir the dry ingredient mixture from 2 into the butter mixture until well incorporated.

5: Add the egg, buttermilk and vanilla extract to the mixture and beat until smooth. Add the walnuts and stir for several seconds.

6: Divide the batter evenly between the two pint-sized Mason jars. Place the jars on a cookie sheet and bake in the oven for 35 to 40 minutes. You know the brownies are done when you insert a toothpick into the middle and it comes out clean.

7: Carefully remove the jars from the oven using an oven mitt. Place on a cooling rack. Set the lid on top of each jar and secure closed with the ring.

8: Let the brownies cool for several hours. Store the brownies in a jar in a dark, cool location. If giving as a gift, decorate with dollies, decorative fabric or ribbon.

Chapter III: Soup-in-a-Jar Mason Jar Gift Recipes

AAAAAAAAAAAAAAAAAAAAAAAAAAAAAAAAAAAAAAAAAAAAAAAAA

Recipe 9: Five Bean Meatless Soup Mason Jar Gift Mix

This ingredient-heavy soup mix makes a great home warming gift. And because it makes 4 gift jars, you can give it to multiple people.

Yield: 4 Gift Jars

Cooking Time: 20 minutes

List of Ingredients:

- 1 pound pinto beans
- 1 pound split peas
- 1 pound kidney beans
- 1 pound northern beans
- 1 pound black beans
- 1 tsp. rosemary, dried
- 1 Tbsp. ground black pepper
- 1 Tbsp. paprika
- 1 Tbsp. dry mustard
- 2 Tbsp. garlic powder
- 2 Tbsp. dried oregano

- 2 Tbsp. salt, table or sea
- 4 bouillon cubes, vegetable
- 8 bay leaves
- 4 Mason jars, quart-sized

AAAAAAAAAAAAAAAAAAAAAAAAAAAAAAAAAAAAAAAAAAAAAAAAAA

Instructions:

1: Add 2/3 cup of each type of bean to each jar. Each Mason jar should have 2/3 cup of each bean. Shake the jars gently to mix the beans together.

2: Place the bay leaves and bouillon cubes to the side for the moment.

3: In a bowl, mix the paprika, ground black pepper, dried onions, salt, oregano, garlic powder and dried rosemary together.

4: Fill 4 sandwich baggies with 3 Tbsp. of the spice mixture from 3. Add two bay leaves and a bouillon cube in each baggie.

5: Place each baggie on top of the bean-filled Mason jars. Attach the lid and ring to the jar.

6: Attach the following directions on the jar:

1. Bring 4 cups of water to a boil.
2. Remove the baggie from the Mason jar. Open the baggie and dump the contents into the boiling water. Continue to boil until the bouillon cube is completely dissolved.
3. Reduce heat and dump the remaining contents of the Mason jar into the water. Let simmer until the beans are soft.
4. Remove from heat and spoon into bowl. Serve warm.

Recipe 10: The Texas Two Soup Mason Gift Jar

This Tex-Mex soup mix makes a great dinner for the fall season and, when placed in a Mason jar, even better gift.

Yield: 1 Gift Jar

Cooking Time: 15 minutes

List of Ingredients:

- 1 (1.61-ounce) brown gravy dry mix package
- 2 Tbsp. chili powder
- 2 tsp. oregano, dried
- 1 tsp. cumin, ground
- 1 tsp. minced onion, dried
- ½ tsp. garlic salt
- 1 ¼ cups pasta shells
- 12 crushed tortilla chips
- 1 Mason jar, pint-sized with wide-mouth

AAAAAAAAAAAAAAAAAAAAAAAAAAAAAAAAAAAAAAAAAAAAAAAAAAAA

Instructions:

1: Dump the gravy mix package into the Mason jar. Place the jar to the side for the moment.

2: Combine the chili powder, garlic salt, dried oregano, minced onion and ground cumin together in a small bowl. Pour this mixture into the Mason jar so that the layer of spices is on top the gravy mix layer.

3: Add the crushed tortillas directly on top of the spice layer. Pour the pasta shells on top of the crushed tortilla chips.

4: Place the lid on the Mason jar and secure closed with the ring. Attach a label to the jar with the below Instructions:

1. Brown and drain 1 pound of ground pork or beef.
2. Fill a pot with 7 cups of water. Place the pot on the stove. Dump the contents in the Mason jar into the water and stir. Bring to a boil.
3. When the water begins to boil, add a can each of diced tomatoes and corn to the pot. Add the drained beef.
4. Reduce the heat to medium and simmer for 30 minutes. Serve warm with sour cream, tortilla chips or shredded cheese.

Recipe II: Classic Chicken and Noodle Recipe Mix Mason Jar Gift

This gift jar mix is perfect for that family member or friend who is not feeling that well.

Yield: 1 Gift Jar

Cooking Time: 10 minutes

List of Ingredients:

- 4 cups egg noodles
- 2 Tbsp. granule chicken bouillon
- 1 tsp. ground black pepper
- 2 Tbsp. dried minced onion
- 2 tsp. dried celery
- Mason jar

AAAAAAAAAAAAAAAAAAAAAAAAAAAAAAAAAAAAAAAAAAAAAAAAAA

Instructions:

1: Place the dried minced onions in the Mason jar. Add the chicken bouillon, black pepper and dried celery. Add the egg noodles on top. Secure the jar closed.

2: Attach the following cooking instructions to the jar:

1. Add 3 to 4 cups of water to a pot. Place the pot on the stove and bring to a boil.
2. Reduce heat and dump the contents of the Mason jar into the pot. Stir.
3. Let the mixture simmer until the noodles are soft.
4. Dish into bowls and serve warm.

Recipe 12: Potato Soup Mason Gift Jar

The potato soup mix added to the Mason jar will warm the recipient up on those cold, winter nights.

Yield: 1 Gift Jar

Cooking Time: 15 minutes

List of Ingredients:

- 2 cups dry instant potatoes
- 2 Tbsp. chicken bouillon, instant
- 1 ½ cups powdered milk
- 1 tsp. parsley
- ¼ tsp. black pepper
- 1 tsp. garlic powder
- ¼ tsp. thyme
- Mason jar

AAAAAAAAAAAAAAAAAAAAAAAAAAAAAAAAAAAAAAAAAAAAAAAAAAAA

Instructions:

1: Put the instant potatoes, chicken bouillon, powdered milk, parsley, black pepper, garlic powder and thyme is a large Ziploc bag.

2: Shake the Ziploc bag thoroughly for several seconds. You want all the ingredients to be well incorporated.

3: Carefully transfer the mixture from the bag and into the Mason jar. Secure the jar closed with the lid and ring.

4: Neatly write the following instructions on a tag that will be attached to the jar:

1. Fill a large mug, bowl or cup with ½ cup of the potato soup mix.
2. Add 1 cup of boiling water to the mug, bowl or cup and stir until smooth.
3. Enjoy!

Recipe 13: Lentil and Curry Soup Mason Jar Gift Mix

This curried lentil mix is a great way to fill your stomach while warming your body during those chilly days and nights.

Yield: 1 Gift Jar

Cooking Time: 10 minutes

List of Ingredients:

- 1 dried Chile pepper
- 2 bay leaves
- 1 ½ tsp. curry powder
- 2 tsp. turmeric
- 1 cup red lentils
- 1 cup yellow lentils
- 5 tomatoes, sun-dried
- Mason jar

AAAAAAAAAAAAAAAAAAAAAAAAAAAAAAAAAAAAAAAAAAAAAAAAA

Instructions:

1: Place the bay leaves in the bottom of the Mason jar. Add the dried Chile pepper. Add the turmeric on top, followed by a layer of curry powder and the 5 tomatoes.

2: Pour ½ cup of yellow lentils into the Mason jar. Place ½ cup of red lentils on top of the layer of yellow lentils. Add the remaining ½ cup of yellow lentils followed by the remaining ½ cup of red lentils.

3: Place the lid and ring on the jar. Include the following directions attached to the jar:

1. Melt 3 Tbsp. of butter over medium heat in a large pot. Crush four garlic cloves and add them and a diced onion to the pot. Let the garlic and onion sauté for 5 minutes.
2. Pour 7 ½ cups of water into the pot. Add the contents of the jar and stir for several seconds. Let the mixture simmer for an hour. You want the lentils to be soft.
3. If necessary, add a bit of salt to taste. Dish into bowls and serve warm.

Recipe 14: Hearty Mason Jar Soup Mix

If you want a hearty soup that warms and feels you up, look no further than this yummy mix.

Yield: 1 Gift Jar

Cooking Time: 10 minutes

List of Ingredients:

- 1/3 cup beef or chicken bouillon cubes
- ½ cup split peas
- ¼ cup onion flakes
- ¼ cup barley
- ½ cup pasta, such as shell or elbow macaroni
- ¼ cup rice
- ¼ cup lentils
- Spiral pasta
- 1 Mason jar, quart-sized

AAAAAAAAAAAAAAAAAAAAAAAAAAAAAAAAAAAAAAAAAAAAAAAAAA

Instructions:

1: Set the Mason jar on the counter and layer the above ingredients in the following order: bouillon cubes, onion flakes, split peas, shell or macaroni pasta, barley, lentils, rice and spiral pasta.

2: Attach the lid and ring to the Mason jar.

3: Attach the following directions to the jar:

1. Brown a pound of beef. Drain thoroughly and set to the side.
2. Scoop the spiral pasta out of the Mason jar and set to the side.
3. Fill a large pot with 12 cups of water. Set the pot on the stove and dump the contents of the Mason jar into the water.
4. Turn the heat on high and bring the water to a boil. Reduce heat and simmer for 35 to 40 minutes.
5. Pour the spiral pasta into the soup and simmer for an additional 15 minutes. Stir in the browned beef from 1 and serve warm.

Chapter IV: Cookie Mason Jar Gift Recipes

AAAAAAAAAAAAAAAAAAAAAAAAAAAAAAAAAAAAAAAAAAAAAAAAA

Recipe 15: Butterscotch Cookie Mix Mason Jar Gift

This gift jar recipe requires only 3 inexpensive ingredients. Despite its simplicity, this gift jar will bring a smile to the face of the recipients.

Yield: 1 Gift Jar

Cooking Time: 5 minutes

List of Ingredients:

- 1 (11 ounce) package butterscotch morsels
- 1 (15.25 ounce) box yellow cake mix
- Quart-sized Mason jar

AAAAAAAAAAAAAAAAAAAAAAAAAAAAAAAAAAAAAAAAAAAAAAAAA

Instructions:

1: Dump the package of yellow cake mix into the jar. Add the butterscotch morsels. Write the following directions on a tag or decorative piece of paper that you will attach to the jar:

1. Turn the oven to 350-degrees.
2. Mix 1/3 cup vegetable oil with 2 large eggs (slightly beaten). Dump the contents of the Mason jar into the eggs/oil mixture and stir until well combined.
3. Let the dough chill in the refrigerator for 15 minutes before dropping the cookie dough by spoonfuls on the baking sheet. Bake for 9 minutes.

Recipe 16: The Best Chocolate Chip Cookie Mix Mason Gift Jar

When you're ever in doubt about what type of cookie to make, look no further than this best chocolate chip cookie recipe. Not only is this recipe Delicious with a capital D, but it also makes a great gift jar!

Yield: 1 Gift Jar

Cooking Time: 10 minutes

List of Ingredients:

- 1 2/3 cups flour, all-purpose
- ½ cup granulated sugar
- ¾ tsp. baking soda
- ½ cup packed brown sugar
- 1 ½ cups chocolate chips, semi-sweet
- Mason jar, quart-sized

AAAAAAAAAAAAAAAAAAAAAAAAAAAAAAAAAAAAAAAAAAAAAAAAA

Instructions:

1: Mix the all-purpose flour with the sugar and baking soda. Pour about a third of this mixture into the jar. Add the semi-sweet chocolate chips and then layer the brown sugar on top. Carefully press the brown sugar down a bit. Add the rest of the flour mixture and attach the lid and ring to the jar.

2: Write the following directions on a label and then attach it to the jar:

1. Turn the oven to 375-degrees.
2. Pour the contents inside the Mason jar into a bowl.
3. In a second bowl, cream together 2 large eggs, ¾ cup butter (softened) and 1 tsp. vanilla. Dump this mixture into the bowl from 2 and combine thoroughly.
4. Use a spoon to scoop the dough into balls onto a baking sheet. Place in the oven for 10 minutes. You want the edges of the cookies to be lightly brown.

Recipe 17: Reese's Cookie Mix Mason Jar Gift

Reese's are a delicious candy made by Hershey's. It is the perfect combination of chocolate and peanut butter. And can be used to create a cookie that your family will crave.

Yield: 1 Gift Jar

Cooking Time: 5 minutes

List of Ingredients:

- 1 box milk chocolate cake mix, super moist
- 1 bag Reese's mini pieces baking chips
- Mason jar, quart-sized

AAAAAAAAAAAAAAAAAAAAAAAAAAAAAAAAAAAAAAAAAAAAAAAAAAA

Instructions:

1: Pour the cake mix into the Mason jar. Add the Reese's pieces on top. Place the lid and ring on the jar and add the following Instructions:

1. Turn the oven to 350 degrees.
2. Mix ½ cup oil with 2 large eggs. Dump the mix from the jar into the bowl and mix with the oil and eggs.
3. Set the dough in the refrigerator for 15 minutes.
4. Spoon the dough into 1 to 2 inch balls onto a baking sheet and back for 8 to 9 minutes.

Chapter V: Bath and Body Mason Jar Gift Recipes

AAAAAAAAAAAAAAAAAAAAAAAAAAAAAAAAAAAAAAAAAAAAAAAAA

Recipe 18: Raspberry Sugar Body Scrub Gift Recipe

Requiring only three ingredients, this sugar body scrub recipe is a great gift for anyone who takes their beauty regiment seriously.

Yield: 1 Gift Jar

Cooking Time: 10 minutes

List of Ingredients:

- 2 to 3 drops raspberry essential oil
- 1 cup granulated sugar
- ½ cup coconut oil, organic
- Mason jar

AAAAAAAAAAAAAAAAAAAAAAAAAAAAAAAAAAAAAAAAAAAAAAAAAAA

Instructions:

1: Mix the raspberry essential oil, sugar and coconut oil together in a bowl. Transfer the mixture into the Mason jar before securing closed with the ring and lid.

Recipe 19: Grits and Honey Exfoliator Mason Gift Jar

This body scrub is perfect for naturally exfoliating the body with

Yield: 1 Gift Jar

Cooking Time: 10 minutes

List of Ingredients:

- ½ cup organic honey
- 1 tsp. sweet almond oil
- ¼ cup grits
- 1 vitamin E capsule

AAAAAAAAAAAAAAAAAAAAAAAAAAAAAAAAAAAAAAAAAAAAAAAAAA

Instructions:

1: Mix together the organic honey, grits and sweet almond oil together the 3 ingredients are well blended.

2: Break open the vitamin E capsule and pour the contents into the honey/grits/oil mixture. Combine all ingredients together.

3: Dump the mixture into the Mason jar and attach the following Instructions:

1. Gently rub the body scrub into wet skin to exfoliate and moisturize. Rinse with warm water and pat dry.

Recipe 20: Sugar and Pineapple Body Scrub

This tropical-like body scrub will remove dead cells to reveal the youthful skin underneath.

Yield: 1 Gift Jar

Cooking Time: 15 minutes

List of Ingredients:

- ½ cup fresh pineapple, pureed to a smooth consistency
- 1 ½ cup granulated sugar
- ½ cup organic coconut oil
- Mason jar

AAAAAAAAAAAAAAAAAAAAAAAAAAAAAAAAAAAAAAAAAAAAAAAAA

Instructions:

1: Mix the purred pineapple with granulated sugar and the organic coconut oil.

2: Transfer the tropical body scrub into the Mason jar. Secure closed with the lid and ring.

Recipe 21: Minty Green Tea Body Scrub Gift Jar

The cool mint in the scrub energizes while the green tea helps keep skin looking fresh and young.

Yield: 1 Gift Jar

Cooking Time: 10 minutes

List of Ingredients:

- 2 Tbsp. organic olive oil, light
- 1 cup granulated sugar
- 2 Tbsp. organic honey
- 3 Tbsp. Epsom salts
- 2 mint tea bags
- 2 green tea bags
- 4 drops vitamin E oil
- 6 drops spearmint essential oil
- Mason jar

AAAAAAAAAAAAAAAAAAAAAAAAAAAAAAAAAAAAAAAAAAAAAAA

Instructions:

1: Mix the Epsom salt with the granulated sugar. Dump the contents from the mint and green tea bags into the salt/sugar mixture and stir until well combined.

2: Stir in the oil and honey, followed by the vitamin E oil and the essential oil.

3: Transfer the body scrub into the Mason jar.

Chapter VI: Pet Mason Jar

Gift Recipes

AAAAAAAAAAAAAAAAAAAAAAAAAAAAAAAAAAAAAAAAAAAAAAAAA

Recipe 22: Doggie Biscuits Gift Jar

Using a bone-shaped cookie cutter really ties this dog biscuit recipe together. If you don't have a bone-shaped cookie cutter no worries. Any shape will do!

Yield: 1 Gift Jar

Cooking Time: 30 minutes

List of Ingredients:

- 2 cups flour, whole-wheat
- 2 Tbsp. melted butter
- 1 cup grated parmesan cheese
- ¾ cup milk
- Bone-shaped cookie cutter
- Quart-sized Mason jar

AAAAAAAAAAAAAAAAAAAAAAAAAAAAAAAAAAAAAAAAAAAAAAAAAAA

Instructions:

1: Combine the grated parmesan, milk, flour and butter together.

2: Roll the dough onto a floured surface. You want the dough to be ¼-inch thick. Cut cookies out of the dough using the cookie cutter and set on the baking sheet.

3: Bake the dog biscuits for 15 minutes at 375-degrees. Once done, remove from the cookie sheet and let cool before placing the biscuits inside the Mason jar.

4: As an added touch, cut a bone shape from a paper bag and write the name of the dog in the middle of the bone. Attach this tag to the jar with some ribbon.

Recipe 23: Salmon Treats Cat Gift Jar

If you're anything like me, you have a few cats at home that desire their very own treats, such as the following salmon treats.

Yield: 1 Gift Jar

Cooking Time: 25 minutes

List of Ingredients:

- 6 to 7 ounces of canned salmon (in water, not oil)
- ¼ cup dry milk, non-fat
- ½ cup cornmeal
- 1 Tbsp. cooking oil
- 1 large egg
- 1 cup flour, whole-wheat
- 2 Tbsp. water
- Quart-sized Mason jar

AAAAAAAAAAAAAAAAAAAAAAAAAAAAAAAAAAAAAAAAAAAAAAAAAAA

Instructions:

1: Turn your oven to 350 degrees and let preheat.

2: Mix the salmon with the dry milk, cornmeal, cooking oil, egg and water. Stir in the whole-wheat flour.

3: Turn the dough oven onto a floured surface and knead several times before rolling it out. You want the dough to be ¼-inch thick.

4: Cut the dough into bite-size pieces using a pizza cutter. Layer the pieces on a baking sheet and back for 15 minutes.

5: Fill the Mason jar with the cooled cat treats and secure closed with the lid and ring.

Recipe 24: Chicken and Spinach Treats for Cats

This cat treat recipe combines real chicken and fresh spinach to create a yummy and healthy treat your feline will love.

Yield: 1 Gift Jar

Cooking Time: 35 minutes

List of Ingredients:

- 1 cup fresh spinach leaves
- ½ cup steamed chicken thighs, boneless and skinless
- 1 cup oats, quick cooking
- 1 Tbsp. catnip
- 1 brown egg
- ¼ cup all-purpose flour
- Quart-sized Mason jar

AAAAAAAAAAAAAAAAAAAAAAAAAAAAAAAAAAAAAAAAAAAAAAAAAAA

Instructions:

1: Make sure the oven is preheated to 350-degrees. Cover the bottom of a cookie sheet with parchment paper.

2: Place the steamed chicken thighs, catnip, egg, oats and spinach leaves in a blender and blend for a few minutes until the ingredients have the same texture as wet sand.

3: Dump the mixture into a bowl. Knead in the flour before rolling the dough out with a thickness of ½-inch.

4: Cut the dough into bite-sized pieces. Place the pieces on the cookie sheet from 1 and bake for about 20 minutes.

5: Fill the Mason jar with the cooled treats.

Recipe 25: Peanut and Carob Dog Treat Clusters Recipe

Carob is a chocolate alternative that you can safely feed to your pooch. You can find carob at various grocery stores both online and off.

Yield: 1 Gift Jar

Cooking Time: 30 minutes

List of Ingredients:

- ½ cup oats
- ½ cup peanuts, crushed
- ½ cup carob powder
- ¾ cup white rice flour

AAAAAAAAAAAAAAAAAAAAAAAAAAAAAAAAAAAAAAAAAAAAAAAAAA

Instructions:

1: Pour the white rice flour into the Mason jar. Follow with the oats, crushed peanuts and carob powder. You want the ingredients to be layered in the Mason jar.

2: Close the jar with lid and ring. Write the following instructions on a tag and attach it to the Mason jar:

1. Cover the bottom of a cookie sheet with parchment paper. Turn the oven on and let preheat to 350-degrees.
2. Dump the ingredients inside the jar into a bowl. Stir in 1 cup of milk.
3. Scoop the dough into 1 Tbsp.-sized clusters and place the clusters on the parchment-covered baking sheet. Bake for 15 minutes. Let cool before giving to your pooch.

About the Author

Molly Mills always knew she wanted to feed people delicious food for a living. Being the oldest child with three younger brothers, Molly learned to prepare meals at an early age to help out her busy parents. She just seemed to know what spice went with which meat and how to make sauces that would dress up the blandest of pastas. Her creativity in the kitchen was a blessing to a family where money was tight and making new meals every day was a challenge.

Molly was also a gifted athlete as well as chef and secured a Lacrosse scholarship to Syracuse University. This was a blessing to her family as she was the first to go to college and at little cost to her parents. She took full advantage of her college education and earned a business degree. When she graduated, she joined her culinary skills and business acumen into a successful catering business. She wrote her first e-book after a customer asked if she could pay for several of her recipes. This sparked the entrepreneurial spirit in Mills and she thought if one person wanted them, then why not share the recipes with the world!

Molly lives near her family's home with her husband and three children and still cooks for her family every chance she gets. She plays Lacrosse with a local team made up of her old teammates from college and there are always some tasty nibbles on the ready after each game.

Don't Miss Out!

Scan the QR-Code below and you can sign up to receive emails whenever Molly Mills publishes a new book. There's no charge and no obligation.

Sign Me Up

https://molly.gr8.com

Made in the USA
Middletown, DE
17 January 2024

47990266R00043